The Earldom Of Mar, A Letter To The Lord Clerk Register Of Scotland, The Earl Of Glasgow

John Thomas Freeman-Mitford Redesdale

In the interest of creating a more extensive selection of rare historical book reprints, we have chosen to reproduce this title even though it may possibly have occasional imperfections such as missing and blurred pages, missing text, poor pictures, markings, dark backgrounds and other reproduction issues beyond our control. Because this work is culturally important, we have made it available as a part of our commitment to protecting, preserving and promoting the world's literature. Thank you for your understanding.

THE EARLDOM OF MAR.

A LETTER

TO THE

LORD CLERK REGISTER OF SCOTLAND,

THE

EARL OF GLASGOW,

BY

THE EARL OF REDESDALE.

LONDON:
JOHN MURRAY, ALBEMARLE STREET.
1883.

LONDON :
PRINTED BY WILLIAM CLOWES AND SONS, LIMITED,
STAMFORD STREET AND CHARING CROSS.

THE EARLDOM OF MAR.

BATSFORD PARK,
January, 1883.

MY DEAR LORD GLASGOW,

THE late Earl of Crawford addressed two volumes of letters to you on the case of the Earldom of Mar in your official character as Lord Clerk Register, and I hope you will not object to receive from me, as one of those who gave judgment in the Committee of Privileges upon it, some observations in reply to his work.

No one who reads it can fail to see that his comments on that decision, and on the jurisdiction of the House of Lords in regard to Scotch Peerage Cases, are influenced throughout by feelings of disappointment at the finding of that tribunal in regard to the claim to the Dukedom of Montrose, which is uppermost in his mind throughout. His research into the question of law on the subject was great, and his opinion deserves careful consideration, but some allowance must be made for prejudice.

The claim to the ancient Earldom of Mar affords a singular instance of the manner in which a bold and continued assertion of right during a long period, in the greater part of which the public had little real information on the subject, may gain a hold on public opinion. For between two and three centuries the Earls of Mar have claimed the ancient earldom, showing at the same time by repeated protests against its not being allowed to them, that they have never been recognized as holding it in the Parliament of Scotland before the Union, or in the House of Lords since; and yet none of them have ever dared to make good his claim before the proper tribunal, either before the Court of Session or the House of Lords. The present claimant particularly refused to take the necessary step to prove his right to the ancient earldom when resisting the claim of the present Earl of Mar, and when his doing so would not have been attended with any additional expense. The traditional doctrine of the family has been to go on claiming the ancient earldom and protesting against its not being allowed, in the belief that their right to it would be by degrees very widely accepted, but on no account to attempt to apply for a legal decision on the subject.

I will not say much on Lord Crawford's complaint against the House of Lords as the proper Court for deciding Scotch Peerage Cases. He was satisfied with it when it gave the Earldom of Crawford; it became bad in his opinion when it refused to give the Dukedom of Montrose. The Court of Session for one hundred and seventy years before the Union was the tribunal to which such cases were referred, there being no House of Lords in the Parliament of Scotland. By the Act of Union the privileges of the peers of England were guaranteed to those of Scotland, and no privilege is more prized than that of their being the judges of their own rights to be members of the House of Lords. For more than one hundred and seventy years since the Union they have decided many very important claims, and Lord Crawford is the first who has objected to their continuing to do so. As to the fitness of the tribunal to determine matters of Scotch law in regard to decisions of the Court of Session, the strong feeling evinced by Scotland in favour of the House of Lords as their Court of Final Appeal, when its jurisdiction was attacked by high authority and was in great danger, may be quoted confidently against Lord Crawford's opinion.

The Earldom of Mar from the earliest date up to the death of the last heir male without issue in 1377, had been inherited uninterruptedly in a male succession. The first question to be determined is whether it then became extinct or went to heirs general.

As to the legal presumption of Scotch peerage law in regard to the remainder in cases in which no instrument of creation appears, the opinion of the great Lord Mansfield, a Scotchman, as given in the Sutherland case, is entitled to great weight. On that occasion he said: "I take it to be settled, and well settled, that when no instrument of creation or limitation of honours appears, the presumption of law is in favour of the heir male, always open to be contradicted by the heir female upon evidence shown to the contrary. The presumption in favour of heirs male has its foundation in law and in truth." Lord Crawford sets up his own opinion against Lord Mansfield's, and in like manner objects to judgments given in several peerage cases by Lords Camden, Hardwicke, and Loughborough. To treat such judgments as decisions which are not to be held as authorities, would be very injurious, and attended with serious consequences.

Since the death of the last heir male of the ancient Earldom of Mar no person has been recognized as holding it either in the Parliament of Scotland or in the House of Lords. Lord Crawford does not attempt to show that any Earl of Mar was so recognised. He assumes that they were so, though all, or nearly all, protested against their not being so, and it is an established fact that every Erskine who claimed it had a safe seat under the Earldom of Mar granted by Queen Mary. Until Mr. Goodeve Erskine proves that he has a right to the ancient earldom, it has unquestionably, so far as legal recognition is concerned, been extinct or dormant for more than five centuries.

Immediately on the death of Thomas, the last heir male, in 1377, the Earl of Douglas, the husband of his only sister Margaret, called himself Earl of Douglas and Mar, and appears so in the Court Roll of Richard the Second in that year; but four years later, in the Rolls of 1381-2, he is Earl of Douglas only, and though he is called Earl of Douglas and Mar in 1383 it is only when mentioned as witness to two charters. Those are the only documents in which he is called Earl of Mar after 1381. The abandonment of the title after having assumed it, and having it recognized in the Rolls of Richard the Second, connected with his mission to another kingdom, where the change would be likely to be noticed, can only be accounted for by his finding that the Earldom of Mar was extinct. This point was not known until the inquiry before the House of Lords, and is not noticed by Lord Crawford, though it is in my judgment.

In two charters of Margaret, after her husband's death, she calls herself Countess of Douglas and Lady of Mar and Garioch, putting these latter titles on a par and inferior to that of Douglas, and in both of these charters her husband is mentioned as Earl of Douglas only. Her second husband John of Swynton was Lord of Mar only.

Margaret died in 1390, and was succeeded in the Comitatus by her only daughter Isabella, the wife of Malcolm Drummond. For twelve years, till his death in 1402, neither he nor his wife called themselves Earl and Countess of Mar, but only Lord and Lady of Mar. His belief in the extinction of the earldom can have been the only reason for his not assuming with his wife the titles of earl and countess. He was brother-in-law to the king, who had married his sister, and could well have maintained his right to whatever he could show his just claim. In Isabella's first charter after his death in 1402, she is only Lady of Mar. The death of Drummond was a violent one. If he had lived some years longer and survived his wife, they would have died Lord and Lady of Mar, without ever having called themselves Earl and Countess. The Comitatus would then have been divided between Sir Robert Erskine, who only claimed half, and Lord Lyle, and the earldom must have sunk into an universally accepted extinction. The sole evidence relied on for the earldom going to a female is Isabella having called herself countess in her charter of 1404. If she had never made such a charter and had died Lady of Mar only, on what would the claim rest?

In Isabella's first charter, after her husband's death, she is Lady of Mar and Garioch. In the following year she calls herself Countess of Mar and Lady of Garioch, and in the following year, in her charter to Alexander Stewart, she is Countess of Mar and Garioch. The latter had ceased to be an earldom on failure of heirs male, and this is fully shown in the proceedings in the Court of Session, where it is treated as a Lordship, and remarkably so in the surrender by Alexander Stewart to King James, in which it is surrendered and re-granted to him as a Lordship only, though held by him from Isabella calling herself countess. Probably Alexander knowing that the Earldom of Mar had become extinct on the death of the last heir male, considered it expedient to get Isabella to treat the earldom of both it and Garioch as open to female inheritance. But whatever may have led to its assumption, it unquestionably did not exist, in regard to the latter, and affords evidence of the careless manner in which the illegal use of titles was treated in those lawless times.

Did the charter of 1404 confer an Earldom of Mar on Alexander Stewart, though it failed to give an Earldom of Garioch? It has been shown for many years after Isabella inherited the Comitatus she did not consider there was an earldom attached to it, and there is nothing in the charter to show that there was an earldom connected with or granted by it. During the twenty-two years from 1404 to the surrender and re-grant of the Comitatus in 1426, there is no record of Alexander having ever sat in Parliament as Earl of Mar, and from the high position he held, from his calling himself Earl of Mar and Garioch, and being recognised as such by the Regent, the Duke of Albany, his uncle (as unscrupulous a man as himself), and from the manner in which he was employed by him, this is a matter to be noticed, and is probably to be accounted for by his knowledge that his right to the earldom would be challenged if he offered himself as such in Parliament. The presumption of law was that it had become extinct on the death of the last heir male, and this is supported by the fact that Isabella herself, during the far greater part of the time she held the Comitatus, while she was the wife of an honest man, never called herself countess, nor her husband earl. That Alexander had no legal right to the earldom is strongly confirmed by the charter of re-grant of the Comitatus on his surrender for the purpose of getting the remainder for his natural son in 1426, in which he is called Alexander Stewart only as having surrendered, and the same in the re-grant. The king desired that it should be shown that the old earldom was no longer attached to the Comitatus, at the same time granting a new one with remainder to the natural son. After that transaction there is a record of Alexander having sat in Parliament.

Alexander Stewart died in 1435, and his son having died before him the Comitatus went to the Crown under the conditions of the last mentioned charter. From that time six Lord Erskines sat in Parliament under six sovereigns without claiming to be admitted as Earls of Mar, and during that period the Crown created several Earls of Mar, to the charter of one of which the Lord Erskine of the day was one of the witnesses. If the earldom under any of those creations had been inherited, and had been in existence when Queen Mary gave an earldom to Lord Erskine, would it have been that of Mar? The undisputed admission of the extinction of the peerage during the period above-mentioned, must be looked upon as a settlement of the question which it would be very dangerous to disturb.

We now come to the manner in which Queen Mary dealt with the earldom. In 1562 she granted the Comitatus with an earldom to her natural brother James, to whom a few days before she had granted the Comitatus of Moray without an earldom, and there is strong evidence as to the extinction of the old Earldom of Mar in her selecting that title for her natural brother's peerage, he being the child of Lord Erskine's sister.

Lord Erskine seeing that this would put an end to his ever becoming Earl of Mar, got his natural nephew to surrender it, who was accordingly made Earl of Moray, sitting as such on the 18th of October, having sat as Earl of Mar on the 10th of September in 1562, the year of the creation of both the earldoms. Is it possible that the queen could have thought, or that it was the general opinion at the time, that Lord Erskine had a right to the old earldom when she created a new one in favour of his natural nephew?

Three years later, on the 23rd of June, 1565, she restored the Comitatus to Lord Erskine in a charter in which she acknowledged him to be heir to Isabella, and that he and his ancestors had been unlawfully deprived of the Comitatus. Lord Crawford holds that the ancient earldom was given to Lord Erskine by the charter restoring the Comitatus. The House of Lords has decided that soon after that restoration he became Earl of Mar by a new creation. I shall enter into this question more fully in discussing the proceedings before the Commissioners for the Decreet of Ranking.

In treating these proceedings Lord Crawford finds it necessary to determine that the precedence awarded to the Earls of Angus, Argyle, Crawford, Erroll and Marishall, was on account of certain high offices held by them. In the directions given to the Commissioners there is no notice taken of official rank, and they are required to give rank, place, and precedence according to the antiquity of the writs, documents, and testimonies produced by them, with this special provision, that as regards such persons as should not appear before them by themselves or their procurators, the Commissioners were to set down every man's rank according to that which should be verified, and should proceed according to the special instructions given by His Majesty for this purpose.

Angus and Argyle did not appear before the Commissioners. Their reasons for not doing so are obvious. They could not prove their right to be placed, as they had been accustomed to be, above several other earls, according to the antiquity of their titles, and they knew that under the powers granted to the Commissioners no allowance was to be made on account of any special exception. In the Angus case this was claimed under a grant of uncertain date, by which the first place and vote in Parliament had been granted to the Earls of Angus, which had been confirmed by King James VI. in a charter under the great seal in 1602, only four years before this inquiry. The earl therefore did not appear, and left his placing to be determined as the king might specially instruct the Commissioners. The king would have placed himself in a wrong position towards the earl, if after having so recently confirmed a special grant of an exceptional character, he allowed it to be set aside by a Commission of his own creation. This reservation, therefore, of the royal power to determine precedence, where the peer himself did not appear, was probably made to meet the case of the Earl of Angus.

Argyle did not appear. The date of his creation was below that of some other earls. He held the offices of Master of the Household and Justiciary General, and was probably in some understanding with the king, and therefore did not appear, and by royal favour had the second place assigned to him.

Crawford was placed third: and here Lord Crawford in his work finds himself placed in great difficulty in assigning a reason for his being placed above the Earls of Erroll and Marishall, who held high official rank, his object being to give to those earls official precedence, and to prevent their being placed according to the date of their creations. The Earl of Crawford appeared before the Commissioners and produced an infeftment given by King Robert to the Earl of Crawford of the Barony of Crawford in 1398, and he had place assigned according to that antiquity. Lord Crawford is obliged to admit that the earl held no great hereditary office, and so in order to find a reason other than the antiquity of his earldom for his being placed above Erroll and Marishall, pleads a special exception for himself on account of the Earls of Crawford having been frequently appointed to carry the sword on state occasions. Feeling, however, that this act of favour to an old earl was hardly sufficient to give permanent precedence over such high hereditary offices as Constable or Marishall, if placing was by official rank, he suggests another reason, founded, on the case which, as I have before remarked, pervades and governs all his arguments and reasonings, namely, that a knowledge or belief in the Commissioners that the Earls of Crawford were rightly entitled to the Dukedom of Montrose may have influenced them in placing him as high in the list of earls as possible ! ! ! This suggestion can only be properly called absurd. His placing unquestionably was on account of the antiquity of his earldom.

The evidence on which the ranking of the Earl of Erroll, who was one of the Commissioners, was determined was the production of a charter to which William de la Hay, Lord Constable of the Kingdom, and William Keith, Lord Marishall, were witnesses in 1451, and another charter of 1455, to which William, Earl of Erroll, and William, Lord Keith Marishall, were witnesses, and the finding of the Commissioners is : " So he was made earl between the years 1451 and 1455."

In the case of the Earl Marishall, who was also one of the Commissioners, the same sort of evidence is relied on, reference being made to the last-mentioned document in Lord Erroll's case, in which he was Lord Keith in 1455, and another document of 1458, in which he was Earl Marishall, and the Commissioners find, " So he was made earl between the years 1455 and 1458."

Can there be any doubt that the rank and place of precedence awarded in the Decreet to these two earls was according to the date of their creations, which, from their inability to produce the charters of their earldoms, were placed on other evidence at periods between three and four years in each case, and consequently that of the Earl of Erroll has always been accepted as of 1452, and of Marishall as of 1456. The object of Lord Crawford in giving official precedence to these earls and not according to the antiquity of their peerages, is to enable him to claim a precedence of 1404, the date of Isabella's charter, for Mar, which he could not do if the rank of Erroll and Marishall, below whom he is placed, was held to have been awarded in accordance with the dates thus assigned to the creation of their earldoms. His whole case in his protests and letters depends on 1404 being the precedence allowed to Mar in the Decreet of Ranking.

The three earls placed next in succession to the abovementioned five are Sutherland, Mar, and Rothes. The Earl of Sutherland produced a charter of 1347, which, if it had been accepted by the Commissioners, would have placed him above Crawford, whose evidence dated from 1398. The Earl of Mar produced a charter of 1404, which, if accepted, would have placed him above Erroll and Marishall. The Earl of Rothes produced a charter of 1459, and was placed next below Mar.

In the Sutherland case there is considerable difficulty in determining the reasons which induced the Commissioners to place him after Crawford, Erroll, and Marishall. It appears to me that they declined to accept the charter of 1347, produced by the earl as evidence of the earldom held by him, believing that the old earldom was not then held by a Gordon, or at all events, considering that without more evidence than was produced before them they would not be justified in declaring that it had been inherited, and was not a new creation.

In the Mar case the earl, in the documents which he placed before the Commissioners, laid a trap to catch the old earldom for himself, or that which would be a foundation for a claim to it at some distant period. The charter which he desired should be accepted as determining his precedence was Isabella's of 1404. If accepted, it would have been declared by the Commissioners that there was an earldom under it to which he, the existing earl, was heir. In like manner, and for a similar reason to that for which they declined to accept the old Sutherland charter, they refused to give Mar the precedence of 1404, placing him after Erroll and Marishall, whose dates of creation, as found by them, were held to be 1452 and 1456, and before Rothes, created in 1459. There are no dates given in the Decreet of Ranking or in the Union Roll, but the precedence allowed to Mar in the Decreet has always been considered to be 1457. It is so recorded and has always been allowed, without objection, in all publications of the Union Roll in which dates are given, and that of 1404 has never been so published in any case. It is important to notice that after the attainder of 1715 had been reversed in 1824, and the Earldom of Mar was again restored to the Roll, the date of 1457 was given to it, after an omission of more than a century, in the Royal Calendar of 1825, which must have been after communication with the earl or the authorities in Scotland, and probably with both.

The manner in which the two Earls of Sutherland and Mar were placed in the Decreet strongly supports the opinion I have given, that in both instances the Commissioners declined to accept the charters they produced as determining the precedence claimed by them. Both sought a ranking which could not be accepted without admitting their claim to the earldom, which the charter produced by each was intended to represent, and which the Commissioners did not feel themselves justified in so declaring without further evidence than that which was before them, or which they could command. They, therefore, put them both together in a position which could not be found to be in any way connected with their respective claims in regard to the charters produced by them, their placing having no relation whatever to the dates of either of the charters. Both cases have been inquired into by the House of Lords, and the places thus assigned to them by the Commissioners have, of course, been found to be wrong. After long and careful consideration, with evidence which the Commissioners had not before them, the House has determined that in the Sutherland case the ranking was too low, and in the Mar case too high, but as it has been considered inexpedient to make any alteration in the ranking on the Union Roll, both earldoms are allowed to remain on it in the places found to be erroneous.

I now desire to call attention to the evidence on which Lord Crawford particularly relies for the existence of the ancient earldom, and that it properly belongs to the Erskines. He holds that in Queen Mary's Charter of Restoration of the Comitatus the earldom was necessarily attached to it, and that by that charter Lord Erskine became Earl of Mar. Why, then, did not the earl lay that charter before the Commissioners? If he believed that the earldom was restored by and with it, and that the commissioners must so decide, he had only to produce it, together with the charter of Isabella and the other documents in his possession proving his descent from the daughter of Gratney, to have his right to the ancient earldom recognised and allowed. The only reasonable conclusion to be drawn from his withholding that charter is that he knew that the ancient earldom was held to be extinct, that that which he enjoyed was a new creation of Queen Mary, and that the Commissioners would refuse to admit that the old earldom was restored with the Comitatus in the Charter of Restoration of the 23rd of June, 1565, in which there was nothing as to an earldom by grant or restoration, and the remainder under which was to his heirs and assigns. He feared that if he produced it the Commissioners might be led by it to inquire as to the first sitting of his father as Earl of Mar, and finding that he was Lord Erskine on the 28th of July, and Earl of Mar on the 1st of August in 1565, would have dated his precedence as they did in the Erroll and Marishall cases, and reported: "So he was made earl between the 28th of July and the 1st of August in the year 1565;" and this is what the House of Lords has done.

This opinion is further confirmed by the course pursued by the earl after the award of the Commissioners. He never protested against their not having given him his just precedence. He had got what he wanted in not having the real date of his creation given him, when they refused that of 1404. He carried on his suit before the Court of Session for the recovery of lands which formerly belonged to the Comitatus, and were then held by Lord Elphinstone, and had judgment given in his favour. Lord Crawford says: " The Decreet of the Court of Session in 1626 fully recognises Earl John as representing Gratney, Earl of Mar, the common ancestor of the Countess Isabella and Sir Robert Erskine." Why, then, did he not claim the precedence of the ancient earldom against that awarded by the Decreet of Ranking? If he had a right to lands possessed by another because they belonged properly to the Comitatus, and the Court of Session had so decided, must not the same Court have given him the earldom if it was still attached to the Comitatus? What, but a knowledge on his part, certain to be acquired during the long course of that law suit, that the lawyers of that day would consider that the earldom was not restored with the Comitatus, but had become extinct with the last heir male, could have prevented his applying to the Court for the desired change of his ranking in the Decreet, in like manner as had been sought and obtained from it in the case of Buchan and others?

It is asked why if Queen Mary did create a new earldom is not the charter for it produced? That it is no longer in existence is no proof that it was not granted, and it is remarkable that in the proceedings on the Decreet very few peers presented their charters of creation. It is also to be noticed that when Murray resigned the Comitatus of Mar in the grant of which to him that earldom was especially given, and became Earl of Moray, in the grant of which Comitatus to him no mention had been made of an earldom, that earldom must have been granted to him in a supplemental charter, which is not known to be still in existence. There is thus plenty of evidence to show that charters of creation have not in many instances been preserved, and anyone desirous of making good his claim to the ancient Earldom of Mar would have no reason for being particularly careful in regard to Queen Mary's charter granting a new earldom. It is also possible that in both cases they may have been made earls by belting.

In commenting on Lord Mansfield's dictum as to the legal presumption in favour of male succession in Scotch peerage law, Lord Crawford remarks that Lord Mansfield in the Sutherland case mentioned the Earldom of Mar as one that had gone through females. In so doing Lord Mansfield accepted the conclusion public opinion had generally allowed to the continued assertion of right by the Earls of Mar to the ancient earldom by protest without inquiry. I believe that if Lord Mansfield had attended the case when heard before the Committee for Privileges, he would not only have concurred in their decision, but would have found in the evidence then produced a strong confirmation of his opinion as to the right of male inheritance, and also of many of the other conclusions come to by the other great law lords of his day, which Lord Crawford considers erroneous.

The prejudice which rules so strongly throughout Lord Crawford's volumes, prevented his making any allowance for the changes which time has introduced into peerage law in Scotland as well as in England. His holding that Queen Mary in 1565 gave an ancient earldom by tenure in a charter in which no mention was made of the earldom granting a Comitatus to one of the co-heirs general of a family which had held it in direct male descent from the earliest times to the death of the last heir male, the ancestor of which co-heir had never claimed more than one-half of the Comitatus, which during the two preceding centuries had been granted with new earldoms to others by special provisions, is a doctrine which it is evident the earl who appeared before the Commissioners for the Decreet of Ranking in 1606 knew they would not accept and therefore did not present the charter to them, and on which he was equally satisfied that the law authorities of the seventeenth century in the Court of Session, would come to a similar conclusion.

If the ancient earldom had no legal existence in the seventeenth century it is absurd to contend that it has in the nineteenth. This is the result of the inquiry before the House of Lords.

It appears to me that it would be most disastrous if the House of Lords should accede to Lord Crawford's proposal, and transfer the jurisdiction in Scotch Peerage Cases wholly or even partially to the Court of Session. It is one which has for long been considered to belong essentially to them, and one which they have exercised without dispute in Scotch Peerage Cases since the Union, and if the transfer is made for his reasons, it would lead, as he no doubt intended it should, to the re-opening of settled cases, with much vexation and disappointment. His condemnation of the power of the House in considering that they do not rule cases, but only advise the Crown upon them, is unfounded. By long practice a person claiming a peerage approaches the Sovereign with a petition, and a protection is thus given to the House of Lords that they may not be called upon to try cases unless the law officers of the Crown consider that there is some ground for having the claim investigated. The Report of the Committee of Privileges is not a judgment, and the House may refuse to agree to it, or refer it back for further inquiry and consideration, but when confirmed by the House it has always been considered a judgment and acted upon without royal or other confirmation. The absolute right of the House to determine who has a right to sit and vote in it was most clearly shown on the life peerage question in 1856, when the Queen, by the advice of her ministers, had created Lord Wensleydale a baron for life only, and issued a summons to Parliament to him on that patent. When the House met it was moved: " That a copy of the letters patent purporting to create the Right Honourable Sir James Parke,

Knight, a Baron of the United Kingdom for life, which has been laid on the table, be referred to the Committee for Privileges with directions to examine and report thereon to the House," and the motion was carried by 138 to 105. The Committee for Privileges is a Committee of the whole House, and the question thus brought before it being one in which the privileges of the House were concerned, all peers attended and debated and voted upon it, as on any other question before the House. It was suggested in debate that the judges should be called in to assist, but it was contended that they had nothing to do with the question as to the right to sit and vote, and no motion was made on the subject. After the matter had been inquired into and considered the following resolution was moved in the Committee: "The Committee have agreeably to your Lordships' order examined and considered the copy of the letters patent purporting to create the Right Honourable Sir James Parke, Knight, a Baron of the United Kingdom for life; and they report it as their opinion that neither the letters patent, nor the said letters patent with the usual writ of summons issued in pursuance thereof, can entitle the grantee therein-named to sit and vote in Parliament." To this an amendment was moved to leave out all the words after the word "opinion," and to insert these words: "That the highest legal authorities having concurred in declaring the Crown to possess the power of creating peerages for life, and this power having in some cases been acted upon in former times, the House of Lords would not be justified in assuming the illegality of the patent creating the Right Honourable Sir James Parke, Knight, Baron Wensleydale for life, and in refusing on that assumption to permit him to take his seat as a peer." This amendment was rejected by ninety-two to fifty-seven, and the resolution agreed to. The government, though they continued to object, declined to contest the matter further, and advised Her Majesty to give way by creating Lord Wensleydale a baron by another patent with remainder to the heirs male of his body. It cannot be denied that the House then claimed and maintained the exclusive right to be the only authority to determine who were entitled to become members of it, and it will be a sad change to consent to any arrangement which may transfer any portion of it to any other tribunal. A great constitutional question is involved in any departure from the existing rule.

    I remain,
        My dear Lord Glasgow,
            Yours very sincerely,
                REDESDALE.

Printed by Libri Plureos GmbH in Hamburg,
Germany